OCT 23 2007

WITHDRAWN FROM LIBRARY

D1174232

J
932
Hewitt

The Egyptians

Written by Sally Hewitt

A⁺
Smart Apple Media

This book has been published in cooperation with Franklin Watts.

Editor: Rachel Tonkin, **Designers:** Rachel Hamdi and
Holly Fulbrook, **Picture researcher:** Diana Morris,
Craft models made by: Anna-Marie D'Cruz,
Map artwork: Ian Thompson

Picture credits
Bettmann/Corbis: 15t; Dagli Orti/Art Archive: front cover t; Dagli
Orti/Art Archive/Corbis: 12tr, 16t, 16b; Werner Forman Archive:
6, 7t, 12bl, 17t, 18, 21t; Werner Forman/Corbis: 7b; Hutchison/Eye
Ubiquitous: 8; Ladislav Janicek/zefa/Corbis: 22c; Charles & Josette
Lenars/Corbis: 11t, 14r, 26bl; Paul C. Pet/zefa/Corbis: 20l; Jose
Fuste Raga/Corbis: 22b; Topfoto: 23t, 24, 26cr; Sandro
Vianni/Corbis: 27t; Roger Wood/Corbis: 10, 20r, 25t.

All other images: Steve Shott

With thanks to our models Maria Cheung and Ryan Lovett

Published in the United States by Smart Apple Media
2140 Howard Drive West, North Mankato, Minnesota 56003

U.S. publication copyright © 2008 Smart Apple Media
International copyright reserved in all countries. No part of this
book may be reproduced in any form without written permission
from the publisher.
Printed in the United States

Library of Congress Cataloging-in-Publication Data

Hewitt, Sally, 1949–
The Egyptians / by Sally Hewitt.
p. cm. — (Starting history)
Includes index.
ISBN-13: 978-1-59920-044-6
1. Egypt—Civilization—To 322 B.C.—Juvenile
literature. I. Title.

DT61.H44 2007
932—dc22   2006034721

9 8 7 6 5 4 3 2 1

Contents

The Egyptians

The ancient Egyptians lived near the banks of the Nile River in Egypt. There was plenty of water and good soil for farming. Their **civilization** started in 3100 B.C. and ended in 30 B.C. when Egypt became part of the Roman Empire.

Egyptian civilization

The Egyptians were ruled by a king called a **pharaoh**. They were clever **engineers** who built cities with magnificent palaces, temples, and **tombs**.

The remains of pots, weapons, tools, and jewelry show that they were also skilled craftsmen.

The Egyptians built some buildings that were meant to last forever. They were made of stone. Some still survive today.

6

Trade

Egypt was a wealthy country. Egyptian traders sold their **goods** in Africa, the Mediterranean, and faraway India. They brought back exotic animals, ivory, timber, silk, and perfume.

This Egyptian wall painting shows images of people trading goods and animals.

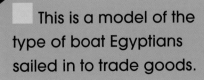

This is a model of the type of boat Egyptians sailed in to trade goods.

The Nile River

The Nile River is the longest river in the world. It runs through the North African desert and out into the Mediterranean Sea.

Floods

Snow melting in the mountains in the south floods the Nile every year in June. The floodwater leaves behind **silt** that makes the soil good for farming.

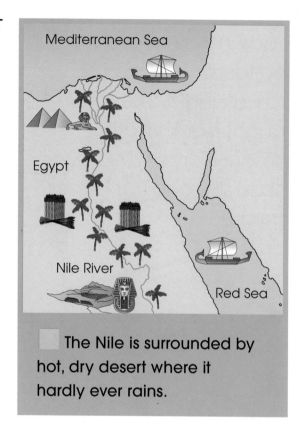

The Nile is surrounded by hot, dry desert where it hardly ever rains.

The Ancient Egyptians used shadoofs to lift water from the canals. Shadoofs are still used today.

Farming

The ancient Egyptians settled along the banks of the Nile River, and farmers planted crops in the rich soil. Their year was divided into three seasons called flood, crop sowing, and harvesting. Because there was little rain, farmers cut **irrigation canals** to carry water from the river to the fields and villages.

Make a shadoof

▶ 1 Tie together three sticks of square dowel, about eight inches (20 cm) long, one inch (2.5 cm) from one end. Spread them into a triangular frame. Press the ends into a modeling clay base.

▶ 2 Loosely tie a 12-inch (30 cm) stick of square dowel, about 2 inches (5 cm) from one end, to the top of the frame.

▶ 3 Add a lump of modeling clay to make a counterweight for the short end.

▶ 4 Use foil to make a small bucket. Hang it from the other end of the lever with a piece of long string.

Try the shadoof. Pull the string down to fill the bucket with water. Push down on the weight to lift the bucket of water.

Egyptian life

Keeping cool and growing enough food to eat were important parts of Egyptian daily life.

Nobles to slaves

Wealthy **nobles** served in the pharaoh's court. Educated **scribes** kept important records, and priests ran the temples. There were many traders and skilled craftsmen, but most people were peasants who belonged to the landowners. There were even a few **slaves**.

Houses were made from mud bricks strengthened with straw and baked hard in the sun. You can still find houses in Egypt made like this.

Houses

Keeping cool was an important part of daily life for the Egyptians. Their houses were built to keep out the heat. The walls were painted white to reflect the sun. Windows were small and high, and vents in the roofs and walls trapped the cool north winds.

After feasting, rich Egyptians enjoyed music. They used fans to cool themselves as they listened.

Food

Rich soil along the Nile meant that Egyptians could grow lots of food for festivals and feasts. Bread and cakes were made from wheat and barley. Figs, dates, and grapes were either eaten fresh, dried and stored, or made into wine. Egyptians caught fish from the river.

Make a fan

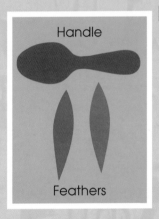

Handle

Feathers

▶ **1** Cut out about 30 feather shapes (left) from thin white cardboard. Make them each about six inches (15 cm) long.

▶ **2** Cut out feathers in gold, purple, and green cardboard, three in each color.

▶ **3** Copy and cut out the handle (above) from strong brown cardboard. Make it eight inches (20 cm) long.

▶ **4** Glue the white feathers onto the back of the handle, adding the colored feathers in between to make a pattern. Use your fan to keep cool.

Clothes

Egyptian clothes were made from **linen**. They were light and loose for keeping people cool in the heat. Men's **kilts** and women's dresses were often pressed into pleats. Farmers wore **loincloths** to work in the fields, while children ran around naked in the heat.

Clothes were usually white, the natural color of the linen cloth, as shown by the Egyptians in this wall painting.

Linen

Linen was made from the fibers of the flax plant. First, the flax heads were removed with a type of comb. Then the stems were soaked, beaten, and combed until they were ready for spinning into thread.

Nets

Nets helped to protect linen clothes from wearing out too quickly. Soldiers wore leather nets over their kilts, and women servants wore beaded nets over their dresses.

This is one of the oldest existing items of clothing. It is an Egyptian linen shirt.

Make Egyptian sandals

The Egyptians wore sandals made from papyrus—a kind of reed that grows on the banks of the Nile.

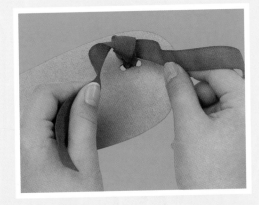

▶ 1 Trace your feet on a piece of thick cardboard. Mark two spots between your big toe and second toe. Mark a spot on either side of your heel.

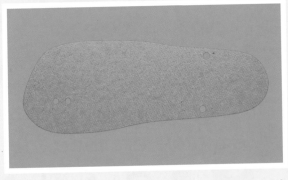

▶ 2 Ask an adult to help you cut out the tracings and punch holes on the marked spots.

▶ 3 Tie two four-inch long (10 cm) pieces of brown ribbon in the holes by the heel, one in each hole.

▶ 4 Thread a 15-inch (40 cm) piece of brown ribbon down and back up through the holes by the toes.

▶ 5 Pull the ribbon so that it is equal lengths, then knot. To make the ribbon go between your toes, tie the ribbon together again two inches (5 cm) along.

▶ 6 Tie the ends of the ribbons in bows around your foot. Finish the sandal for your other foot and try them on.

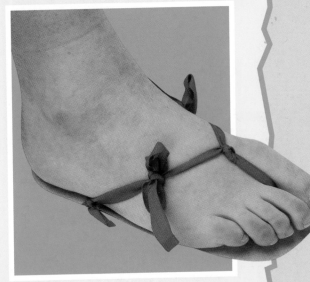

Hair and makeup

Most Egyptians wore some jewelry. Ordinary people wore copper rings and **amulets** to keep away evil spirits. Jewelry for wealthy Egyptians was made of gold from Egypt's own gold mines. Collars, rings, earrings, bracelets, and **anklets** were set with colorful semiprecious stones.

Makeup

The Egyptians used mirrors, combs, tweezers, and makeup to help them look their best. Colored minerals were ground into powder and mixed with wax to make black eye paint and red makeup for lips and cheeks.

Wigs and wax

Egyptians wore long, black, braided wigs. A cone of scented wax worn on top of the head melted in the heat of the day and trickled down the wigs, making them smell nice.

Both men and women outlined their eyes with black makeup.

Craftsmen molded, beat, and carved metal into jewelry, such as this collar.

Make a decorated collar

Decorated collars added richness and color to the Egyptians' plain linen clothes.

▶ 1 Draw the shape of the collar (below). Make it as wide as your shoulders. Punch two holes in the top as shown.

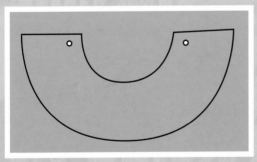

▶ 2 Cut colored straws into one-inch (2.5 cm) lengths. Decorate the collar by painting stripes and gluing on rows of colored straws and sequins to make a pattern.

▶ 3 Thread ribbon through the two holes and tie together. Wear your collar.

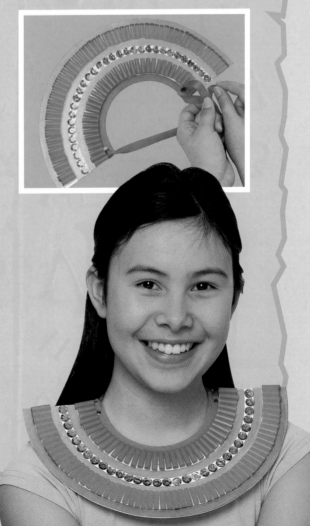

Writing

The ancient Egyptians wrote in **hieroglyphs**. Some of the words looked like pictures. For hundreds of years, historians could not understand the hieroglyphs.

In 1799, the Rosetta stone was found. On it, the same words were written in three different languages: Greek, Demotic, and hieroglyphs. This meant that scholars could now translate hieroglyphs for the first time.

The Rosetta stone unlocked the ancient secrets of the hieroglyphs.

Scribes wrote hieroglyphs on papyrus or carved them in stone.

Scribes

Very few ancient Egyptians could read and write hieroglyphs. There were about 700 signs to learn. Scribes started their training as young boys and spent many years learning to read and write hieroglyphs.

Papyrus

Papyrus was a kind of paper made of pith from the stem of the papyrus reed. Strips of pith were crisscrossed on a frame and flattened under heavy weights to make sheets.

You can see the writing on this ancient piece of papyrus.

Write your name in hieroglyphs

Hieroglyphs were either a whole word or a single letter.

The name of a pharaoh was written on an oval **cartouche**.

▶ Write your name in hieroglyphs and put it in a cartouche.

Gods and goddesses

The ancient Egyptians worshipped hundreds of gods and goddesses. They believed in life after death and tried to make sure they would get to the spirit world. Pharaohs went to a special place called "the land of the gods" when they died.

The gods

Egyptians believed that the gods controlled human beings and all of nature.

The falcon-headed god Re is always shown with a golden disc.

Re was the sun god and creator of men.

Thoth, the moon god of wisdom, had a curved beak of a sacred ibis.

Horus, protector of pharaohs, had a falcon's head.

Anubis was the jackal-headed god of death, rebirth, and **mummification**.

Isis was the goddess of women and children.

Khnum was the ram-headed god of the Nile.

Make a head of the cat goddess Bastet

Re's daughter, a cat called Bastet, was the goddess of the harvest.

▶ 1 Scrunch up some newspaper to make a fist-sized ball. Put it on top of a cardboard tube from an empty roll of toilet paper, and attach it to the tube with masking tape.

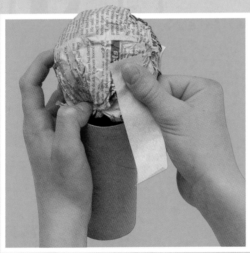

▶ 4 Cover the head and neck with a layer of papier mâché. Leave it to dry thoroughly.

▶ 5 Paint the head dark green all over, but paint the eyes yellow. Paint on gold earrings and a gold jewel on the forehead.

▶ 2 Mix a little craft glue with water in a bowl. Tear up small pieces of newspaper and put them in the bowl to soak.

▶ 3 Shape two thick triangles from glue-soaked newspaper for ears and a strip for the nose. Attach them to the head with papier mâché strips.

The pharaoh

The pharaoh was the king of Egypt. The Egyptians believed that the pharaoh was a god and that his wife was a goddess. A boy born to be the pharaoh learned to hunt, fight, and lead his army in battle. The pharaoh was also a high priest in the temple.

Famous pharaohs

Ramses the Great built many great buildings and monuments, the ruins of which can still be seen today. Similarly, jewelry, clothes, and weapons from the tomb of the pharaoh Tutankhamun tell us a great deal about ancient Egypt.

War

The pharaoh went to war to protect his land against hostile armies or to take over another country. He rode in a horse-drawn chariot and carried a bow and arrow.

A carving of Ramses the Great.

A picture of Tutankhamun riding to war in a chariot.

20

A pharaoh had colored crowns for different occasions. He wore crowns of different colors in different parts of Egypt, and another color in times of war.

This painting on a coffin shows a pharaoh's crown.

Make a pharaoh's blue crown

▶ 1 Copy and cut out the shape of the crown (below) on blue construction paper. Make it about the width of your head.

▶ 2 For decoration, glue on gold spots, a coiled cobra, and a golden sun disk.

▶ 3 Cut a band of gold construction paper to go around your head. Glue the band to the bottom of the blue crown and staple the ends together. Wear your crown.

21

Temple life

Egyptian temples were huge. They were built of stone because they were meant to last forever. Priests performed temple rituals, such as offering gifts to the gods. Only high priests and the pharaoh went into the inner temple. Ordinary people were allowed into the temple courtyard for festivals.

Temple walls were painted and carved with stories of gods and pharaohs.

Around the temple

The temple gate was called a pylon. Statues of the pharaoh stood at the gate. Tall, thin **obelisks** carved with messages to the gods marked the point where the first rays of the sun fell. **Sphinxes** guarded the avenue in front of the temple.

A sphinx had a lion's body and the head of a man.

The hour watcher priest

The hour watcher priest was in charge of making sure the temple rituals were carried out on time. By day, he kept time by the sun. At night, he used a water clock. Water dripped slowly from a hole in the bottom of a special container. It took an hour for water to drop from one mark to the next.

A water clock from ancient Egypt.

Make a water clock

▶ 1 Make a very small hole in the base of a large paper cup with a safety pin (ask an adult to help).

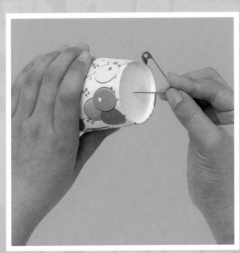

▶ 2 Glue black construction paper around the cup. Decorate it with Egyptian figures and hieroglyphs.

▶ 3 Fill the cup with water and suspend it in a tall glass.

▶ 4 Mark the level of the water every five minutes with a waterproof pen on the inside of the cup. How long does it take to empty?

The pyramids

Egypt's great **pyramids** were tombs for some of the pharaohs and their families. Each pharaoh's body was laid in a chamber deep inside the pyramid to protect it from the heat, from robbers, and from animals. The burial chamber was filled with things the pharaoh would need in the **afterlife**.

The pyramid shape

The shape of the pyramid was built to look like the mound that rose from water at the beginning of time, as told in Egyptian **myths**. The sun god Re stood on the mound's peak and called up all the other gods and goddesses.

The four sides of a pyramid faced north, south, east, and west.

The Great Pyramid

The Great Pyramid at Giza is about 4,500 years old. It was the tomb of King Khufu. The workers building the pyramid had no pulleys, only levers and rollers to move two million blocks of stone. It took about 20 years to build one huge pyramid.

The insides of burial chambers were decorated with pictures and writing.

Make a pyramid

▶ **1** Copy and cut out the pattern (below) of a four-sided pyramid using yellow construction paper. Include a flap on one edge.

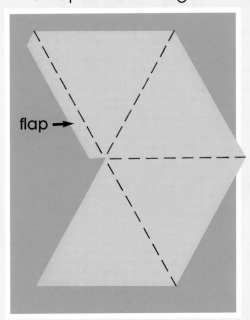

flap →

▶ **2** Fold along the dotted lines. Tuck the flap under and glue it to form a pyramid.

▶ **3** Paint details such as lines for stone blocks on the pyramid. You could also place a small box inside for a burial chamber.

The afterlife

The ancient Egyptians believed in life after death. They thought they would need their bodies in the afterlife, so they took great care to **preserve** dead bodies. This was done by a process called mummification.

Mummification

Mummification was carried out by **embalmers**. The heart was left in the body. The brain was pulled out through the nose with a hook.

This wall painting shows embalmers at work mummifying bodies.

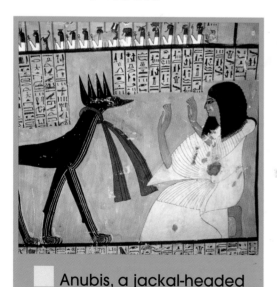
Anubis, a jackal-headed god, was the god of mummification.

The lungs, stomach, intestines, and liver were removed, dried, and put in **canopic jars**.

The body was dried, the face was made up, and a wig was put on.

Then the body was rubbed with scented oil, covered in **resin**, and wrapped in linen.

The canopic jars were protected by the four sons of the god Horus.

This jar has the head of Duamatef, a jackal-headed god.

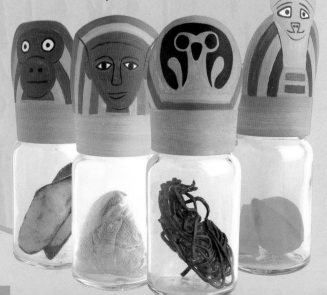

Make canopic jars with dried vital organs

▶ **1** Find four small glass jars. Draw the pictures (below) of the four sons of Horus onto strips of paper. Tape one picture around the top of each jar.

Hapi—baboon-headed god who protected the lungs.

Duamutef—jackal-headed god who protected the stomach.

▶ **2** To make the lungs, cut out shapes of lungs in orange peel and dry them out. For the stomach, blow up a small pink balloon, then let out most of the air.

▶ **3** Make the intestines by painting dried noodles brown and dark red. Take a dried-out, used tea bag or coffee filter and wrap it in plastic wrap to make the liver. Put each organ in its correct jar.

Qebehsenuef—falcon-headed god who protected the intestines.

Imsety—human-headed god who protected the liver.

Glossary

Afterlife
Life after death. The Egyptians believed that they lived on in another place after they died.

Amulet
An object worn to protect against evil spirits.

Anklet
Jewelry worn around the ankle.

Canopic jar
A jar used in ancient Egypt to hold organs of the body.

Civilization
An organized society, usually based around a city.

Embalmer
Someone who treats a dead body to stop it from decaying.

Engineer
A person who designs and builds buildings and machines.

Goods
Things bought and sold such as food, cloth, and jewels.

Hieroglyph
A symbol or picture used for writing. The ancient Egyptians wrote in hieroglyphs.

Irrigation canals
Ditches that carry water from a lake or river to fields where crops grow.

Kilt
A pleated, knee-length skirt.

Linen
Cloth woven from threads spun from the flax plant.

Loincloth
A cloth tied around the hips and between the legs.

Mummification

A way of keeping a dead body from decaying by treating it with oils and wrapping it in cloth.

Myth

A traditional story about gods and heroes.

Noble

Someone with wealth and power in a royal court or government.

Obelisk

A monument in the shape of a flat-sided pillar with a pointed, pyramid-like top.

Pharaoh

A king of ancient Egypt.

Preserve

To keep from decaying or rotting.

Pyramid

A shape with a square base and triangular walls. Some

Egyptian royalty were buried in giant pyramids.

Resin

A sticky tree sap that was used by embalmers in mummification.

Scribe

Someone who writes documents by hand. Ancient Egyptian scribes wrote in hieroglyphs.

Silt

Tiny pieces of mud or clay carried along by rivers. Silt helps to make soil rich for farming.

Sphinx

A creature with a lion's body and the head of a man, a ram, or a bird.

Tomb

A grave, or a cave or building that contains a grave.

Index